PIANO · VOCAL · GUITAR

HAL·LEONARD

WEDDING ESSENTIALS

INCLUDES REFERENCE CD

CHRISTIAN WEDDING FAVORITES

ISBN 978-1-4234-8861-3

HAL·LEONARD®
CORPORATION

7777 W. BLUEMOUND RD. P.O. BOX 13819 MILWAUKEE, WI 53213

Visit Hal Leonard Online at
www.halleonard.com

CHRISTIAN
WEDDING FAVORITES

ANSWERED PRAYER

Words and Music by MIKE JONES
and ANTHONY LITTLE

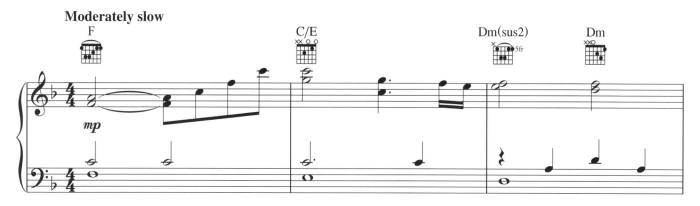

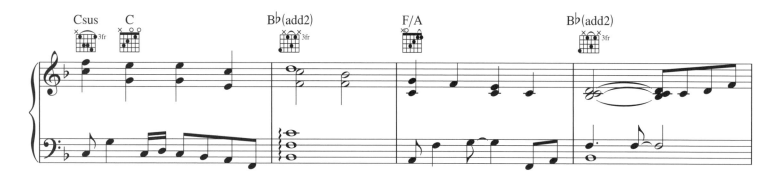

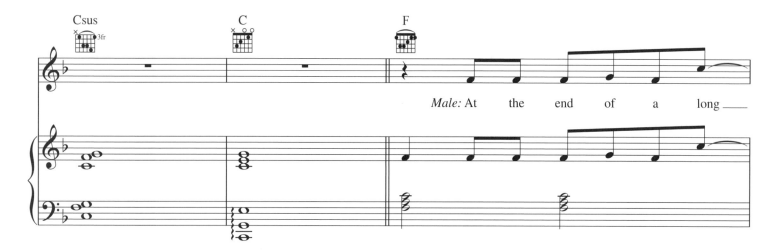

Male: At the end of a long ____

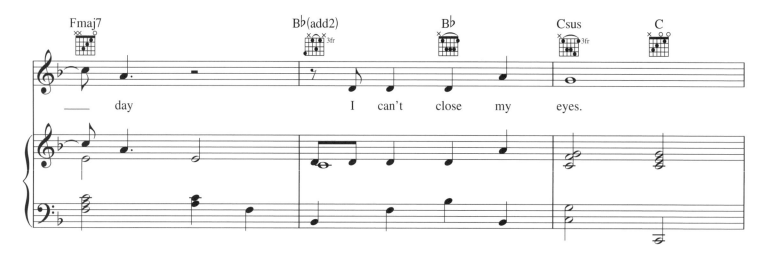

____ day I can't close my eyes.

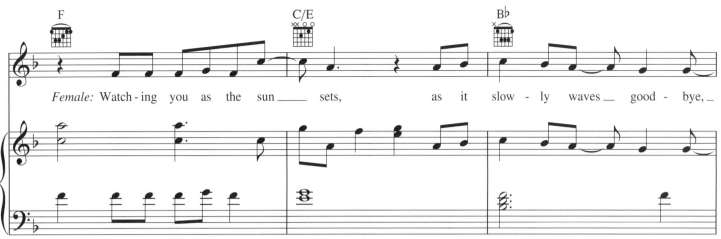

Female: Watch-ing you as the sun ___ sets, ___ as it slow-ly waves ___ good-bye, ___

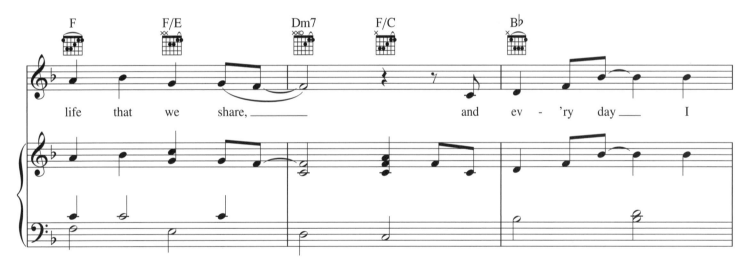

___ it's times like these I thank the Lord for the

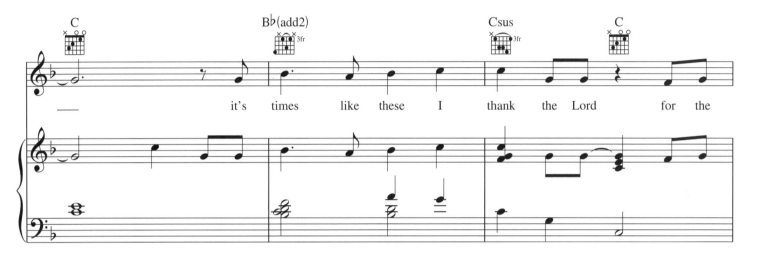

life that we share, _____ and ev-'ry day ___ I

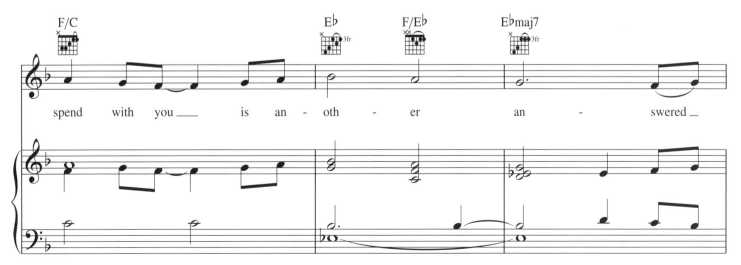

spend with you ___ is an-oth - er an - swered ___

* This phrase is sung both times at written pitch (1st time: high in the male range).
** This phrase is sung both times at written pitch (2nd time: high in the male range).

now that you're here _____
now that you're here _____

Both: our love grows rich -

To Coda ⊕

- er year af - ter _____ year. _____ *Male:* And if

life should end _____ to - mor - row _____ I'd leave a mil - lion - aire, _

8vb

_____ *Both:* 'cause in my heart _____ I'd

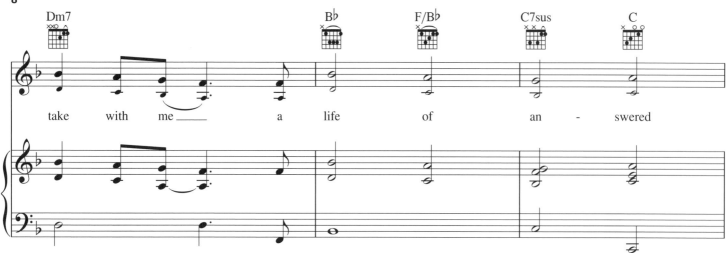

take with me ____ a life of an - swered

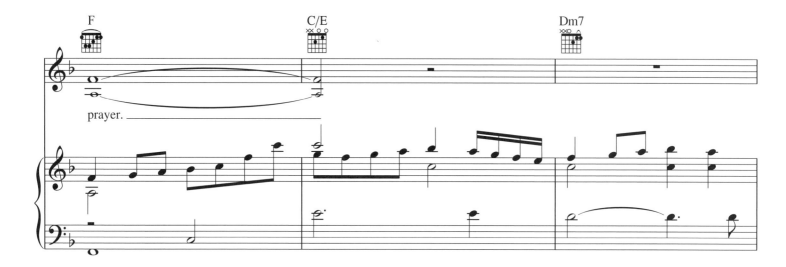

prayer. _____

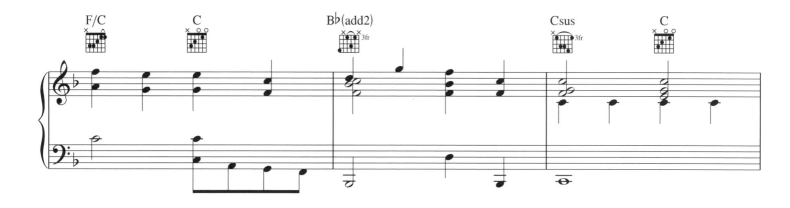

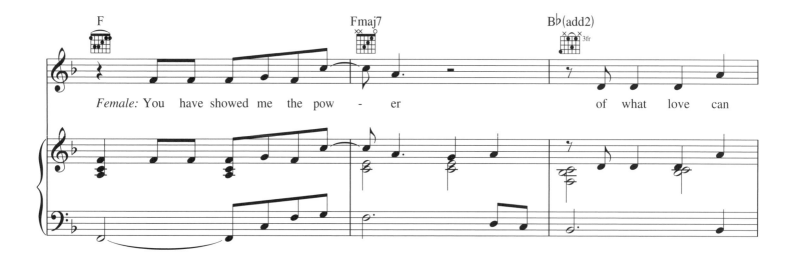

Female: You have showed me the pow - er of what love can

do.

Male: I see glimps-es of heav — en with your

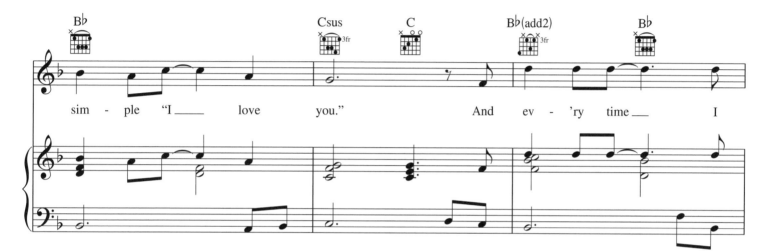

sim - ple "I ____ love you." And ev - 'ry time ____ I

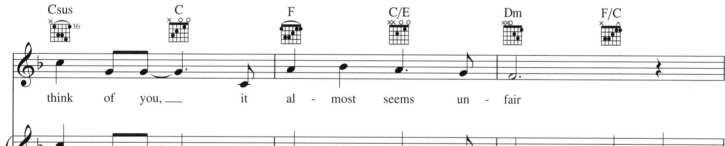

think of you, ____ it al - most seems un - fair

for a man ____ like me to have so man - y

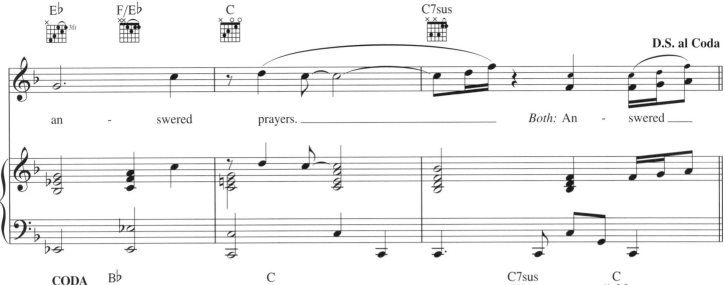

GOD CAUSES ALL THINGS TO GROW

Words and Music by STEVEN CURTIS CHAPMAN
and STEVE GREEN

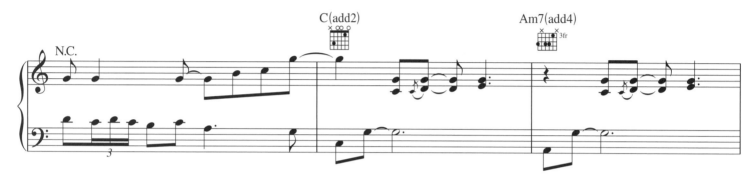

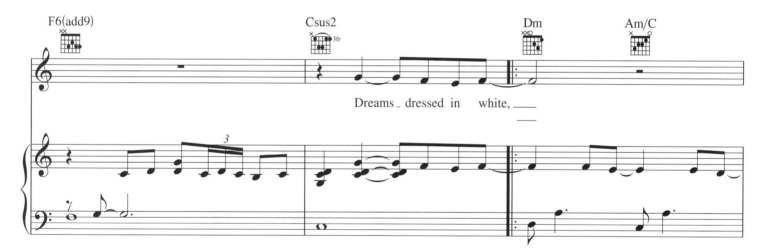

Dreams dressed in white, ___

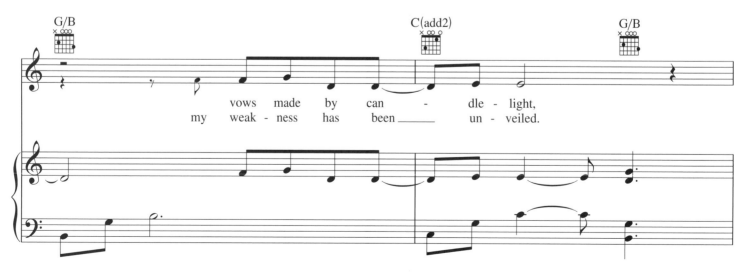

vows made by can - dle - light,
my weak - ness has been _____ un - veiled.

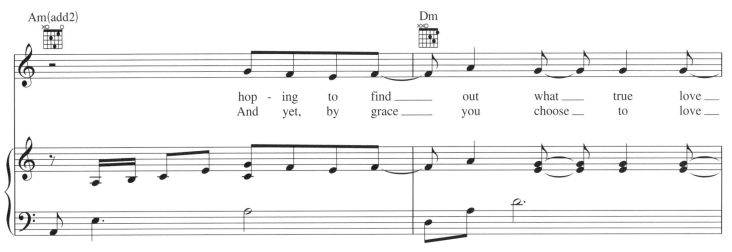

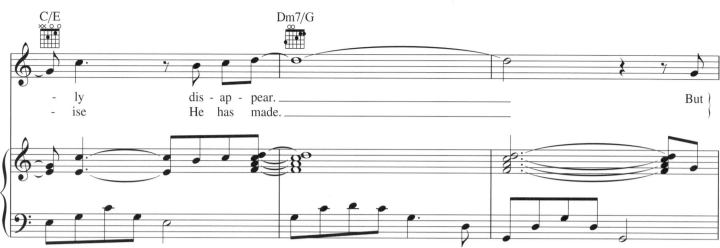

-ly dis-ap-pear. _____ But
-ise He has made. _____

God caus-es all _____ things to grow. _____

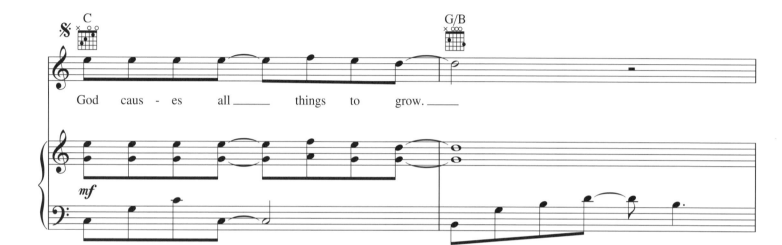

Through ev-'ry sea-son we know _____

He will guard _ the _ life _____ that He's plant-ed in _ our souls. _

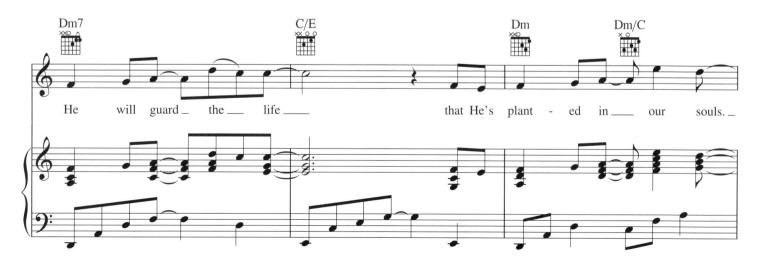

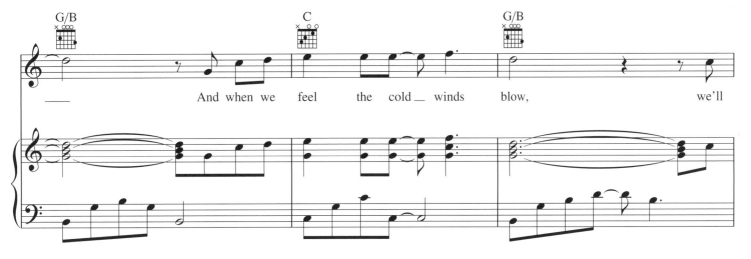

And when we feel the cold___ winds blow, we'll

hold to what___ we know: God caus - es

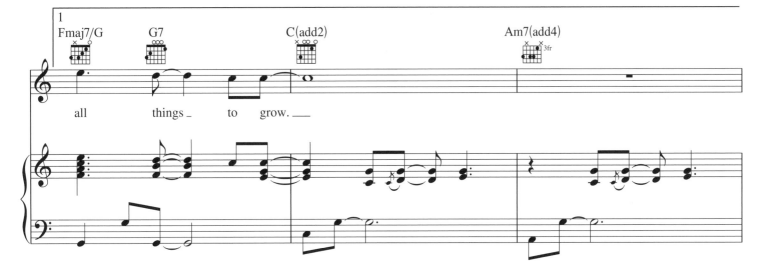

all things___ to grow.___

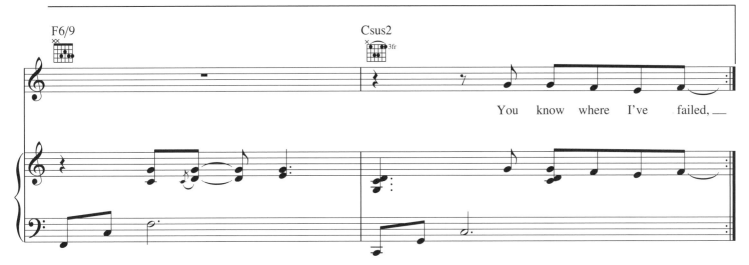

You know where I've failed,___

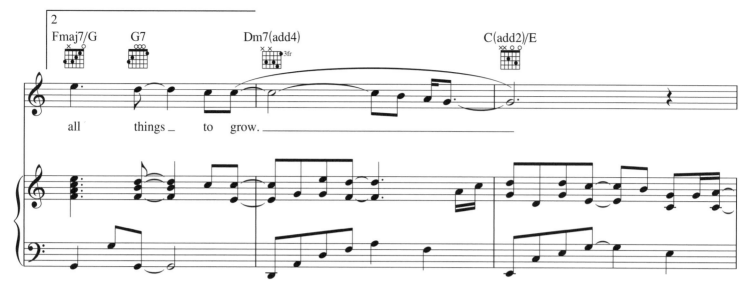

all things ___ to grow. _____

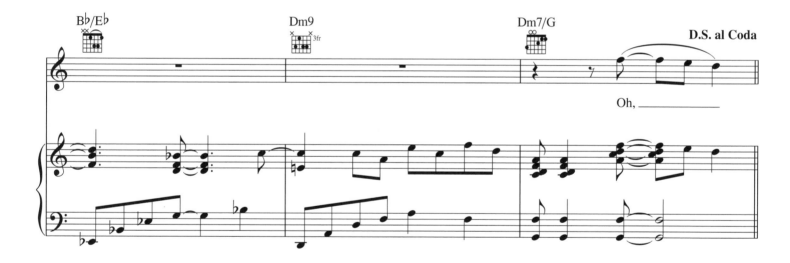

Oh, _____

D.S. al Coda

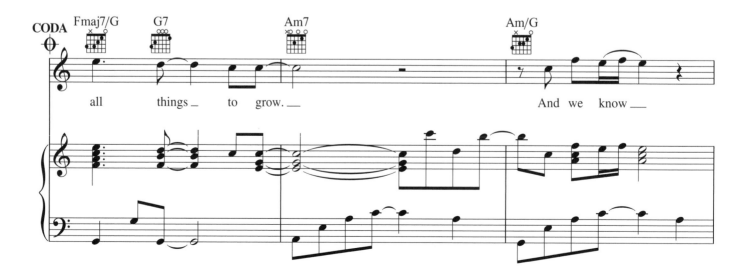

all things ___ to grow. ___

And we know ___

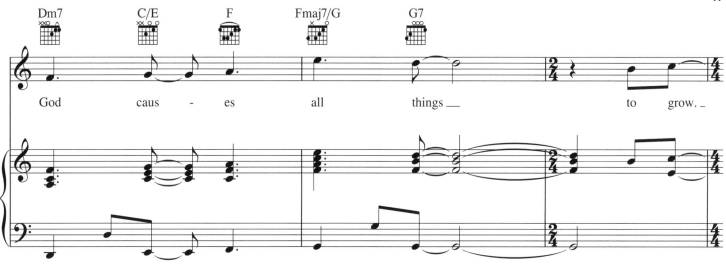

God caus - es all things ___ to grow. ___

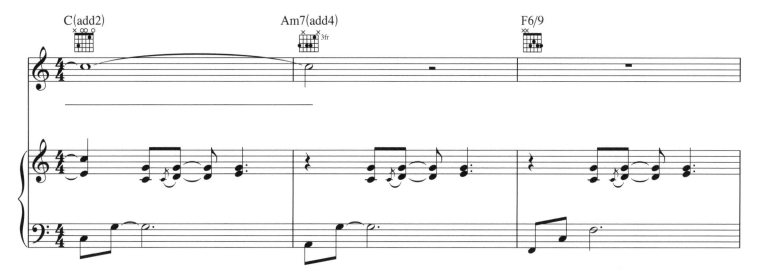

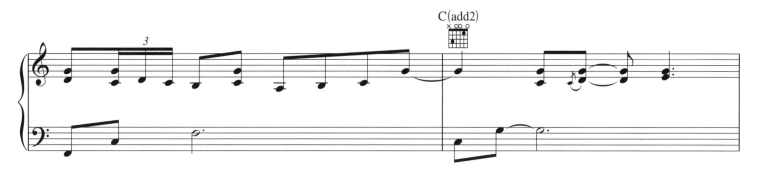

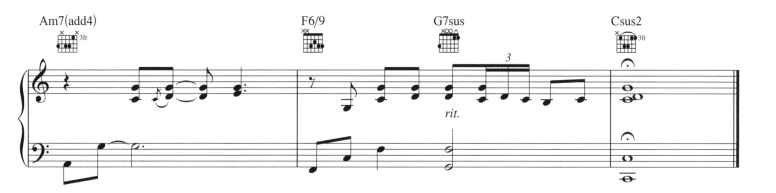

GOD KNEW THAT I NEEDED YOU

Words and Music by
MELODIE TUNNEY

Gentle Ballad

I look at you and I see the one God chose for me.
You know my heart in a way I'm known by no one else.

What did I do to deserve all I have received?
And who you are gives me strength beyond myself.

We're like a hand in glove, one heart made from two.
In spite of all you see, I know your love is true.

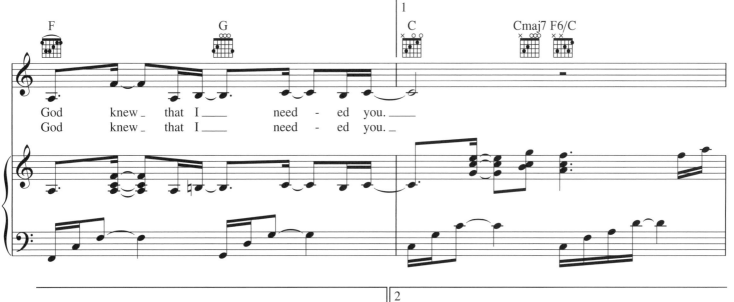

God knew __ that I __ need - ed you. __
God knew __ that I __ need - ed you. __

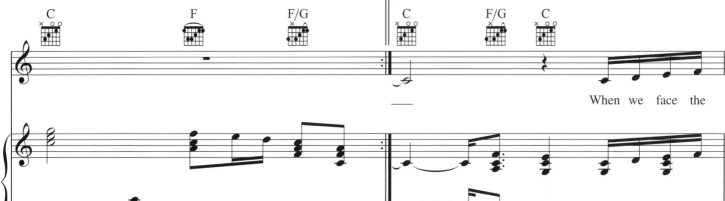

When we face the

dark - est of __ the nights, __ I'll reach out for __ your hand. __ And I know your

love will hold __ me tight __ till we __ can see __ the sun __ a - gain, __ for

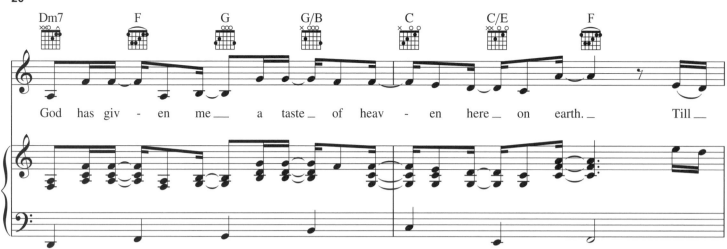

God has giv-en me _ a taste _ of heav - en here _ on earth. _ Till _

life is through, _ I be - long with you. _____

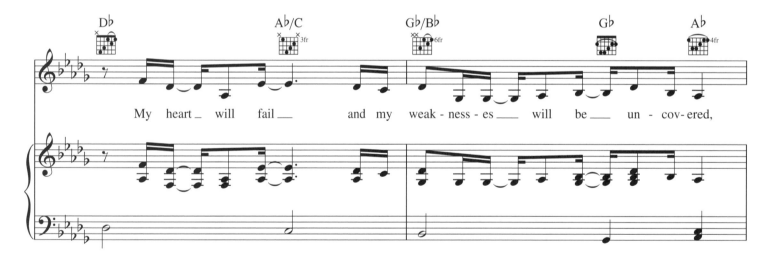

My heart _ will fail _ and my weak - ness - es ___ will be _ un-cov-ered,

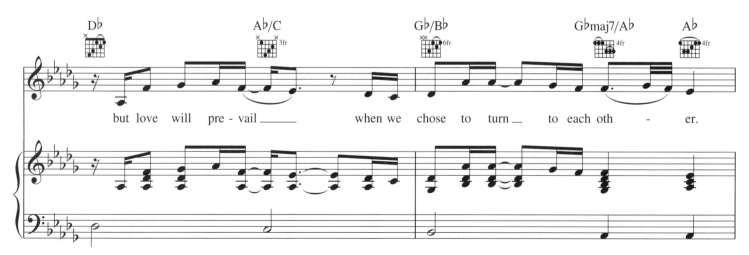

but love will pre - vail _____ when we chose to turn _ to each oth - er.

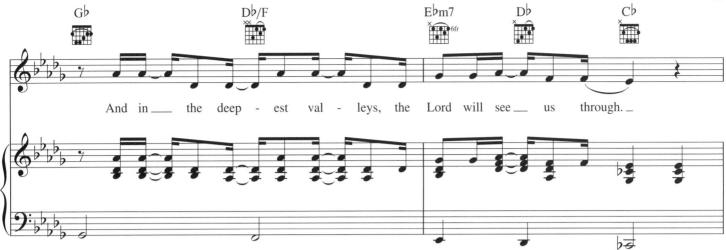

And in ___ the deep - est val - leys, the Lord will see ___ us through. ___

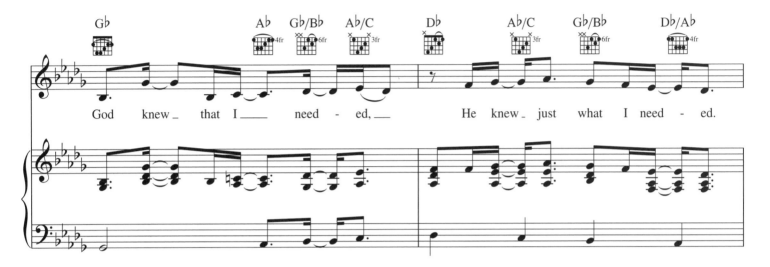

God knew _ that I ___ need - ed, ___ He knew _ just what I need - ed.

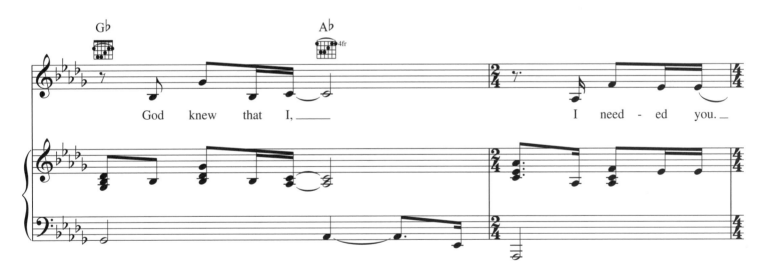

God knew that I, _____ I need - ed you. ___

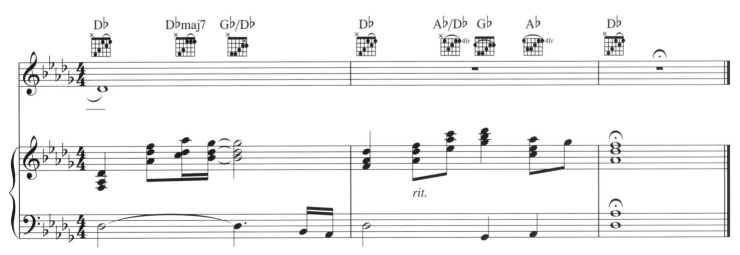

rit.

HOUSEHOLD OF FAITH

Words by BRENT LAMB
Music by JOHN ROSASCO

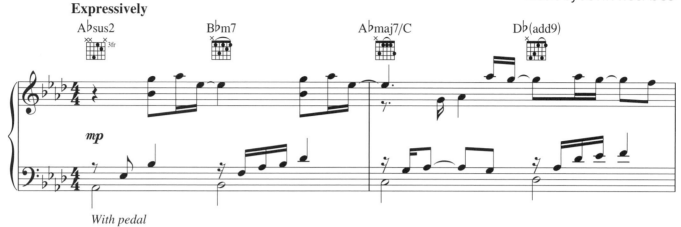

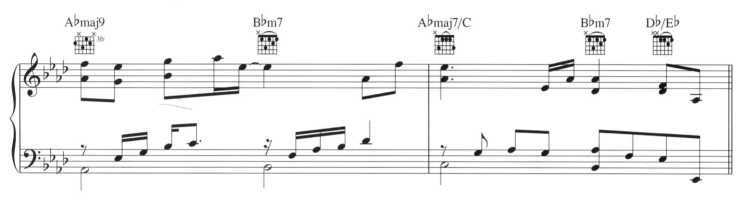

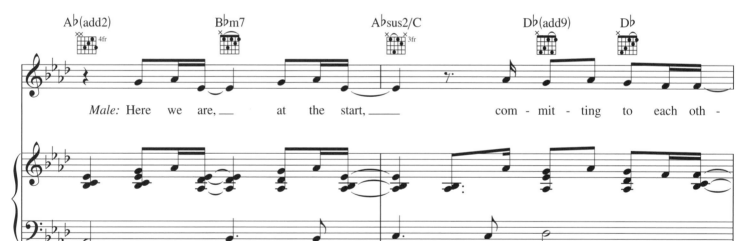

Male: Here we are, ___ at the start, ___ com - mit - ting to each oth -

- er by His Word and from our hearts.

I WILL BE HERE

Words and Music by
STEVEN CURTIS CHAPMAN

Freely

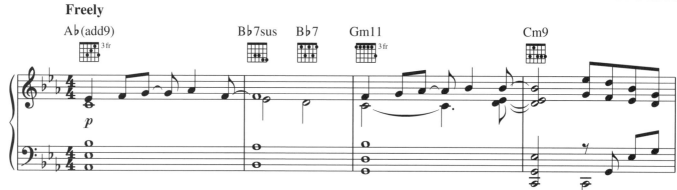

Moderately

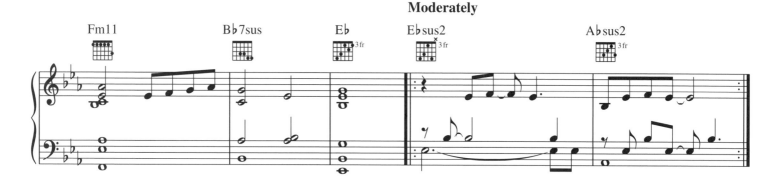

To-mor-row morn-in' if you ___ wake up and the sun does not ___ ap-pear, ___
To-mor-row morn-in' if you ___ wake up and the fu-ture is ___ un-clear, ___

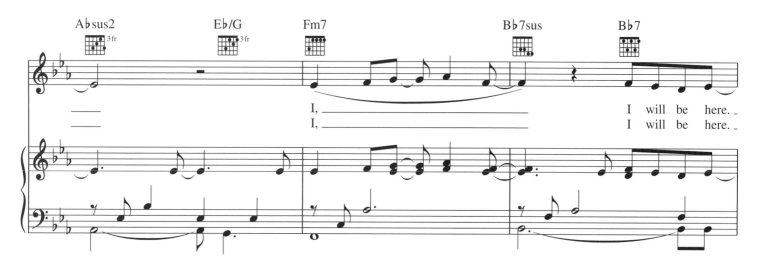

___ I, _____ I will be here.
___ I, _____ I will be here.

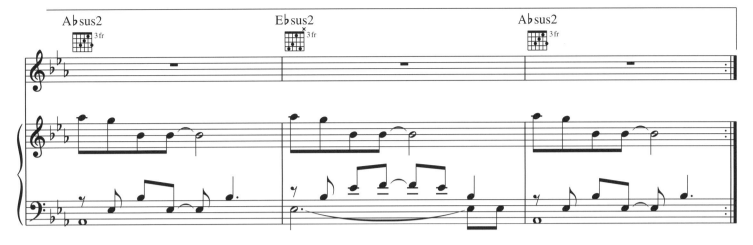

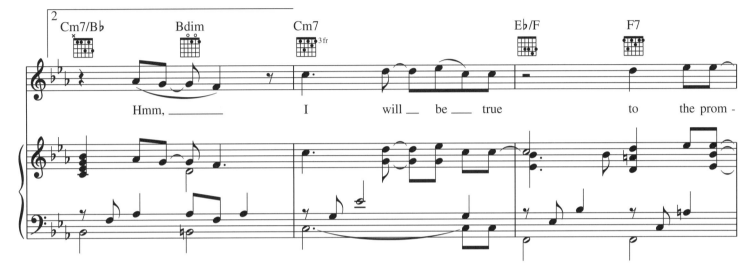

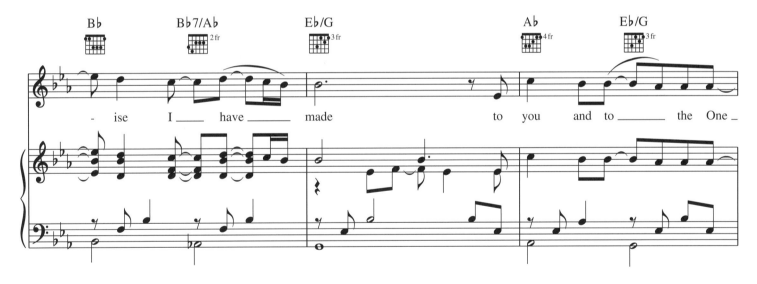

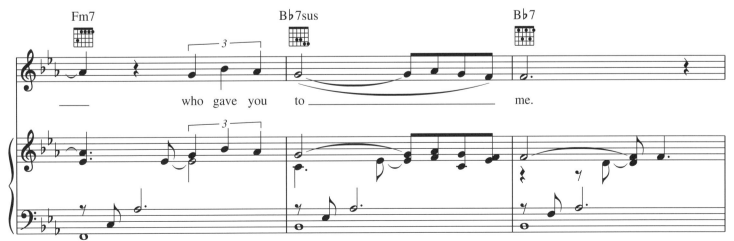

32

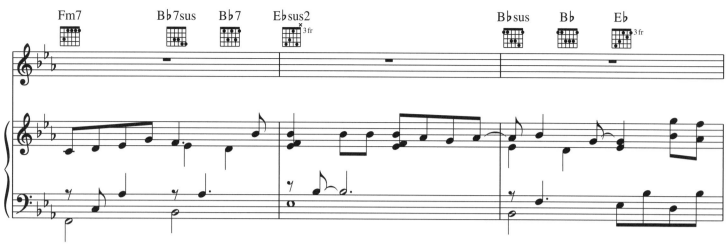

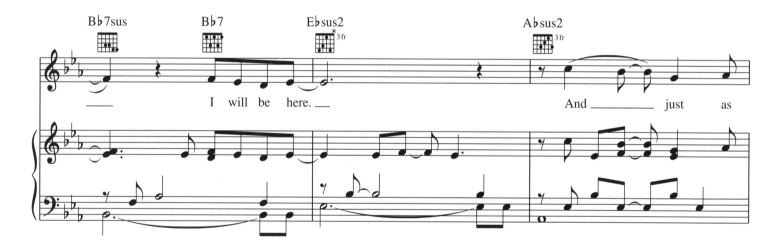

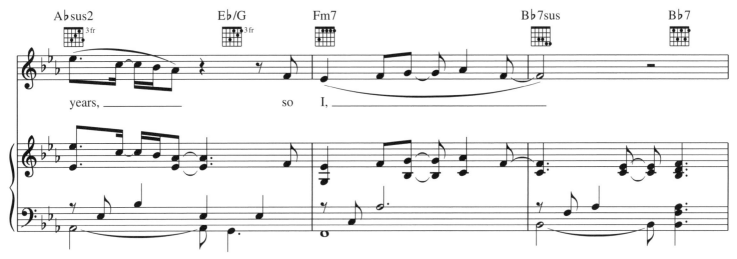

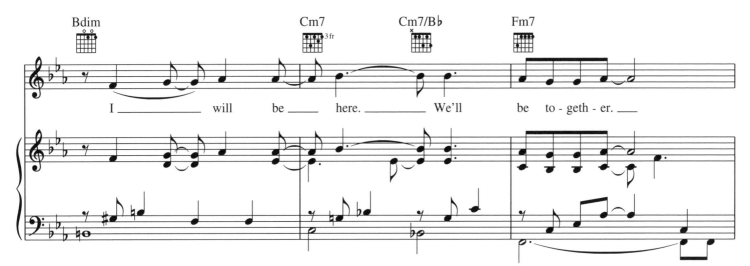

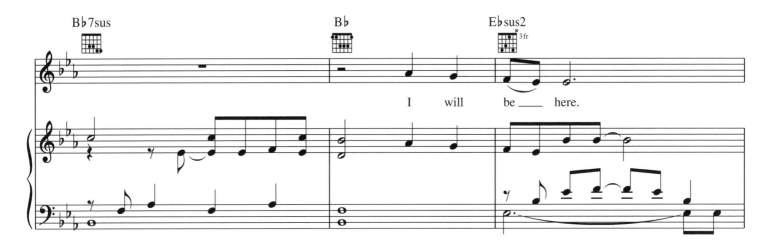

LOVE WILL BE OUR HOME

Words and Music by
STEVEN CURTIS CHAPMAN

Moderately slow, in 2

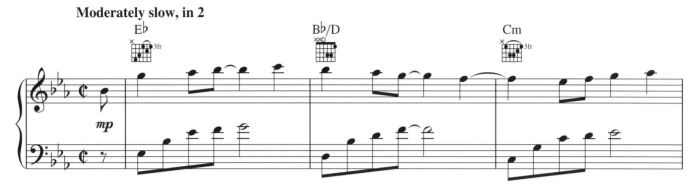

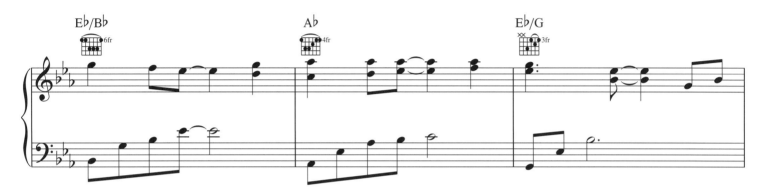

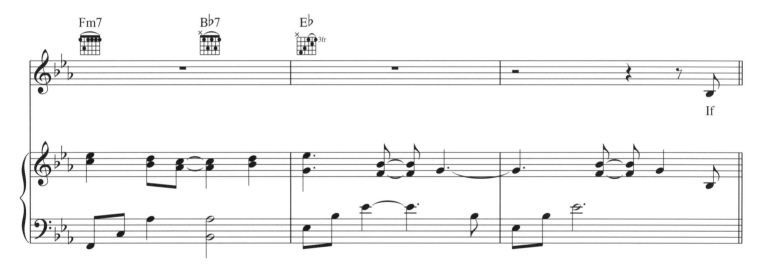

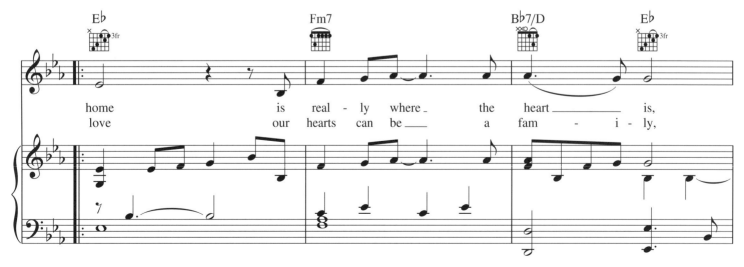

home   is real - ly where   the heart   is,
love   our hearts can be   a fam - i - ly,

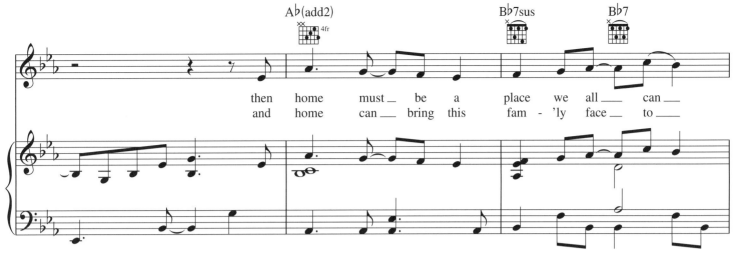

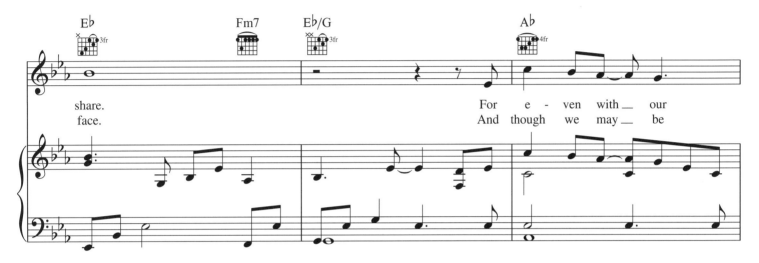

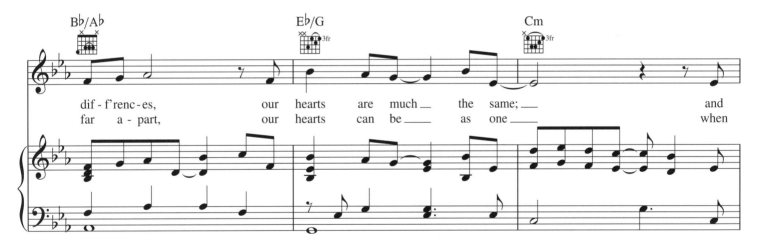

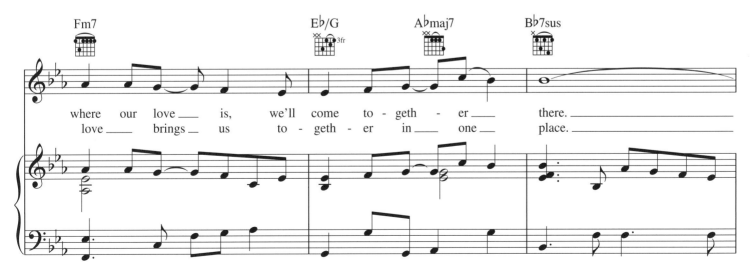

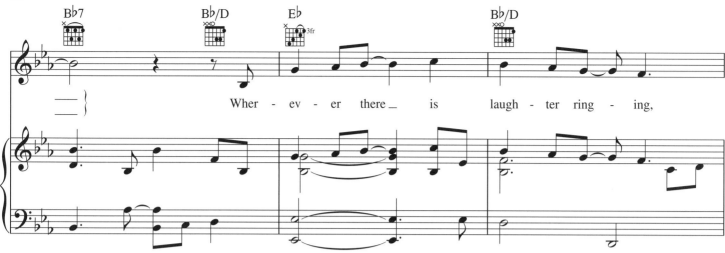

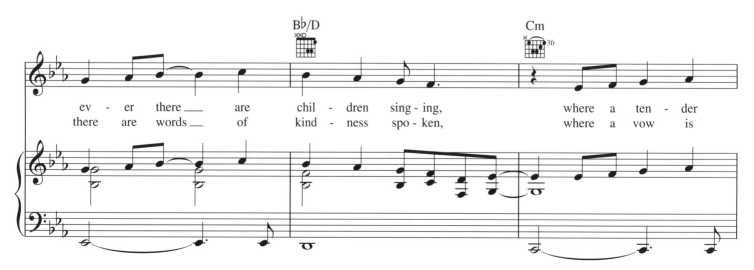

heart is beat - ing,
nev - er bro - ken, } we can live ___ to - geth - er there; ___

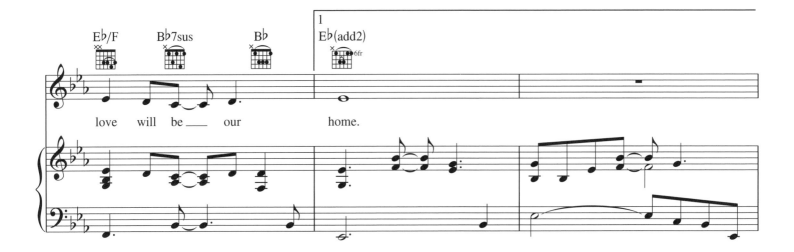

love will be ___ our home.

With home.

Love ___ will, love will be ___ our

home. _____ Love _____ will,

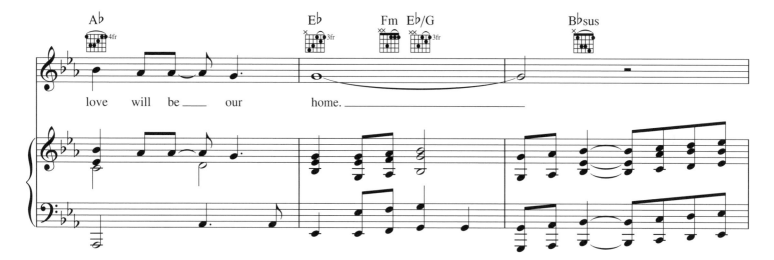

love will be _____ our home. _____

Love _____ will, love will be _____ our home. _____

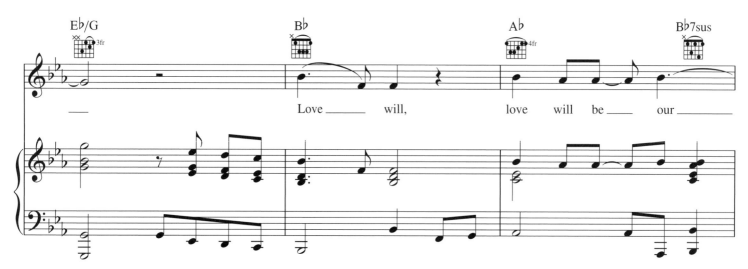

Love _____ will, love will be _____ our

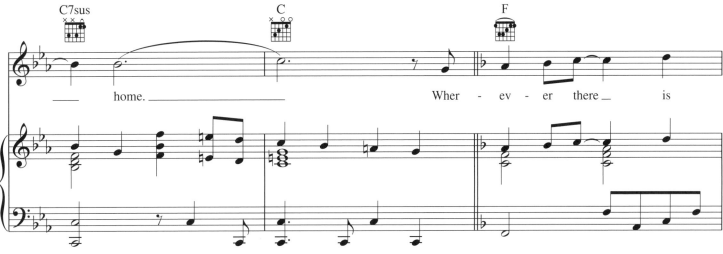

home. Wher - ev - er there ___ is

laugh - ter ring - ing, some-one smil - ing, some - one dream - ing,

we can live ___ to - geth - er there; ___ love will be ___ our

home. Wher - ev - er there ___ are chil - dren sing - ing, ___

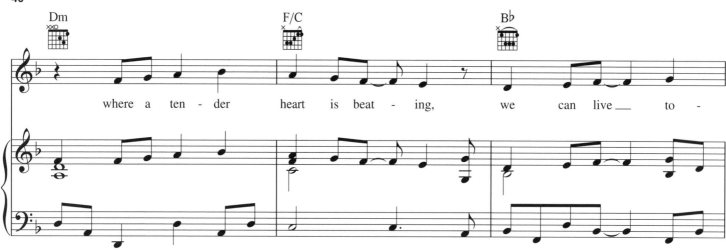

where a ten - der heart is beat - ing, we can live ____ to -

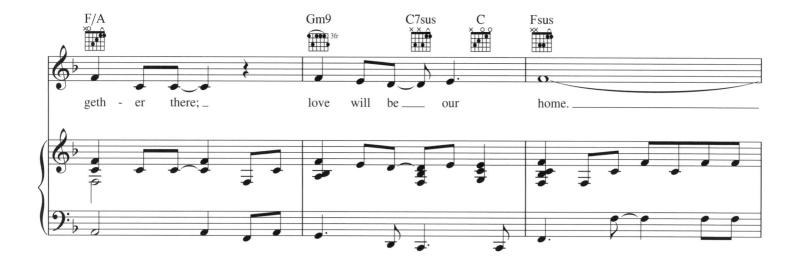

geth - er there; ____ love will be ____ our home. _____

____ Love ____ will, love will be ____ our _____

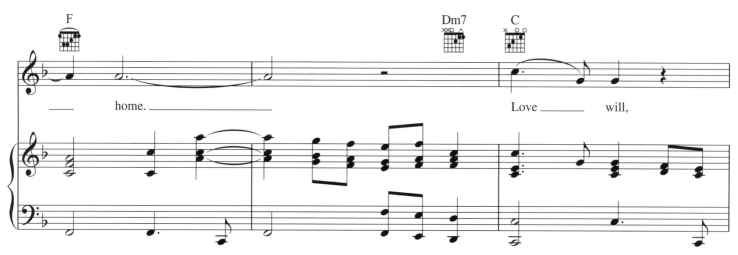

____ home. _____ Love _____ will,

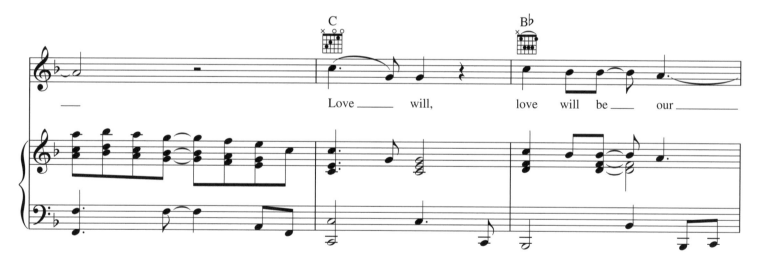

IF YOU COULD SEE WHAT I SEE

Words and Music by GEOFF MOORE
and STEVEN CURTIS CHAPMAN

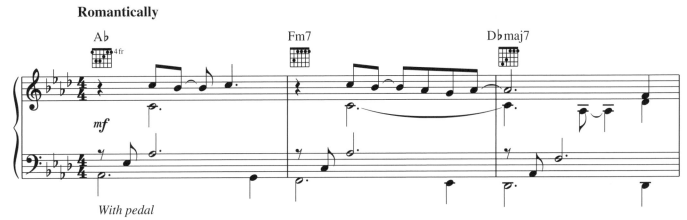

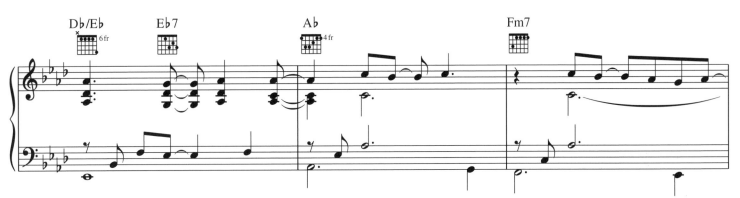

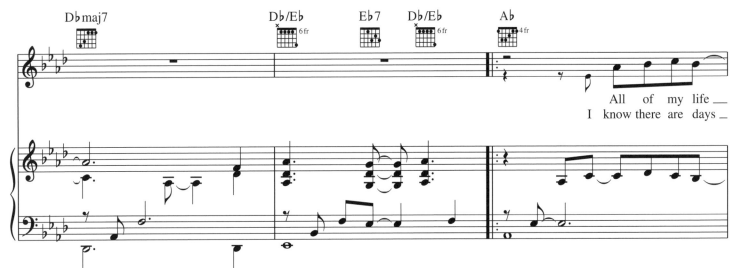

All of my life ___
I know there are days ___

___ I have dreamed ___
___ when you feel _____

that some - how love ___ would find me. ___
so _____ much less ___ than i - deal, ___

the on - ly one ___ for me,

if you could see ___ what I see. ___

then you'd un - der - stand _____

SEEKERS OF YOUR HEART

Words and Music by MELODIE TUNNEY,
DICK TUNNEY and BEVERLY DARNALL

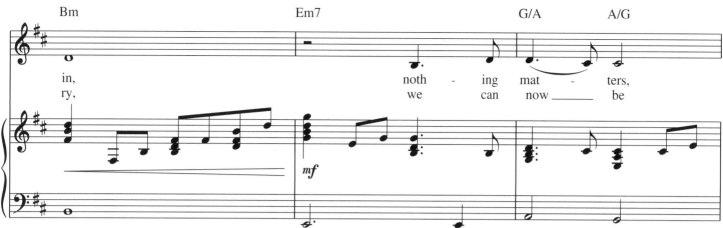

in,
ry,
noth - ing mat - ters,
we can now ____ be

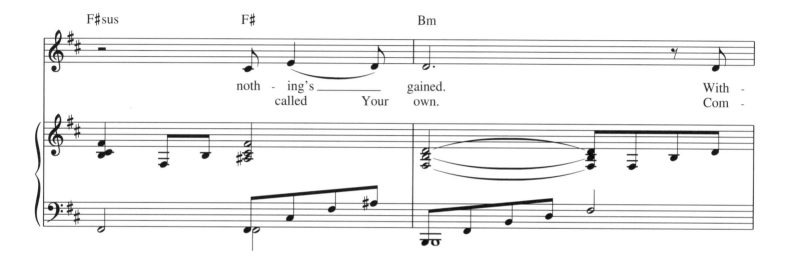

noth - ing's ____ gained.
called Your own.
With -
Com -

out Your ho - ly ____ pres - ence, our lives are lived in
plete ____ cre - a - tions, filled with You a -

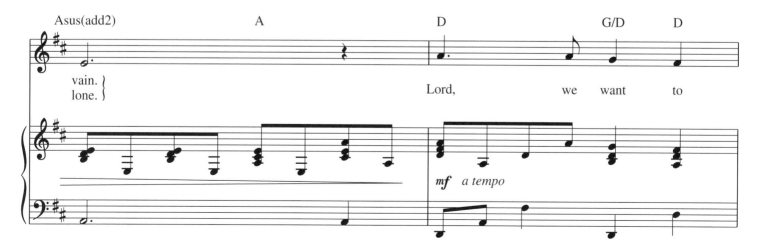

vain.
lone.
Lord, we want to

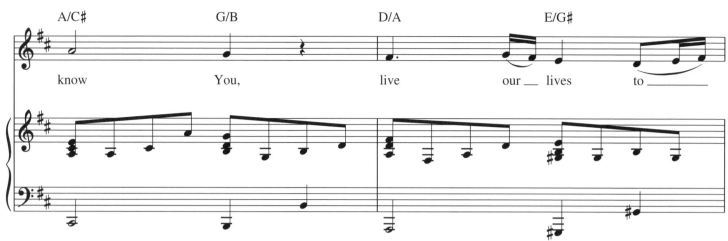

know You, live our __ lives to _____

show You all the love we owe You. We're

seek - ers of Your heart.

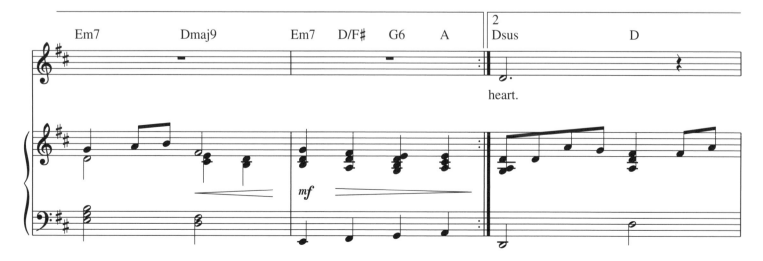

heart.

Lord, we want to know You, live our lives to _____

show You all the love we owe You. We're

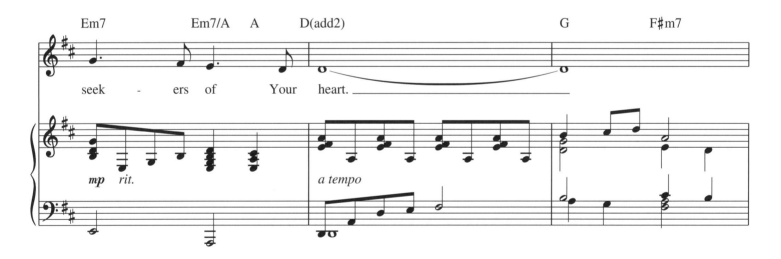

seek - ers of Your heart. _____

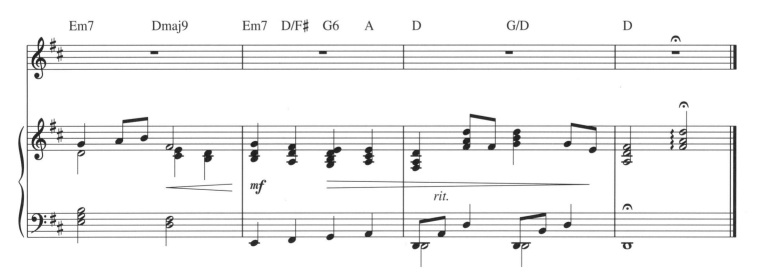

THIS DAY

Words and Music by
LOWELL ALEXANDER

Moderately slow, expressively

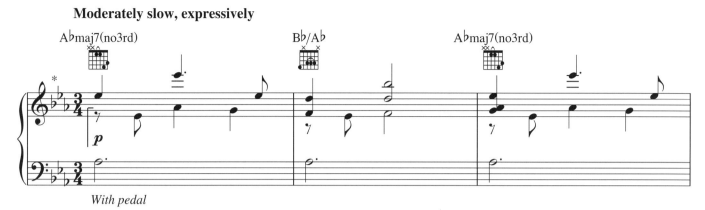

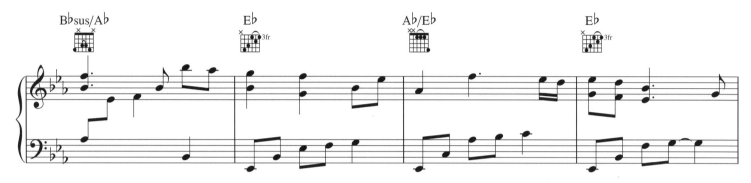

With pedal

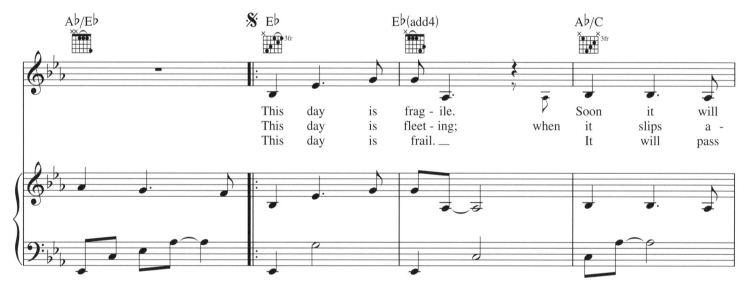

This day is frag - ile. Soon it will
This day is fleet - ing; when it slips a -
This day is frail. __ It will pass

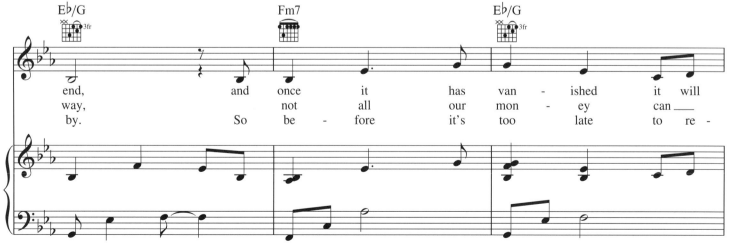

end, and once it has van - ished it will
way, not all our mon - ey can __
by. So be - fore it's too late to re -

* Recorded a half step higher.

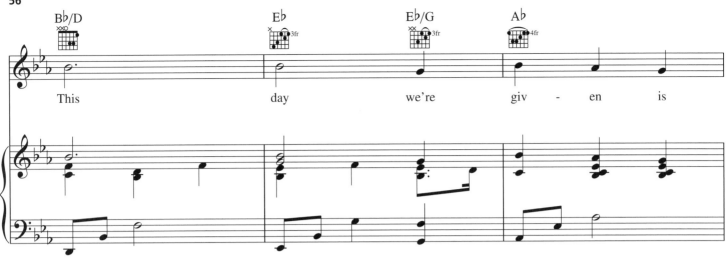

This day we're giv - en is

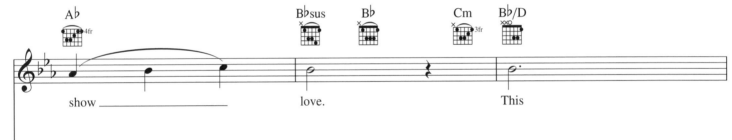

gold - en. Let us

show love. This

day is ours for one mo - ment.

'TIL THE END OF TIME

Words and Music by
STEVE GREEN

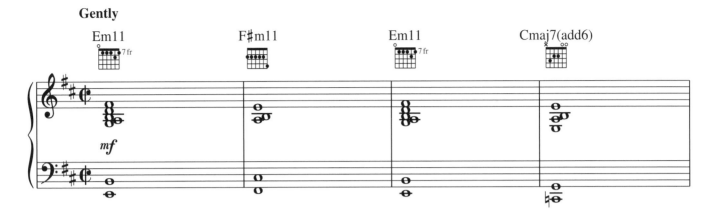

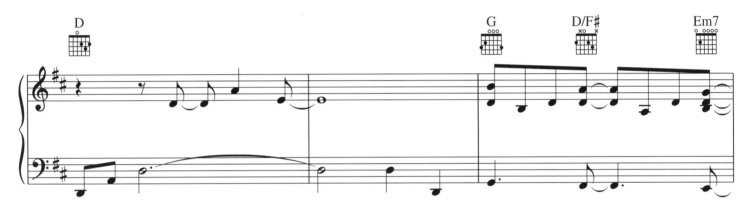

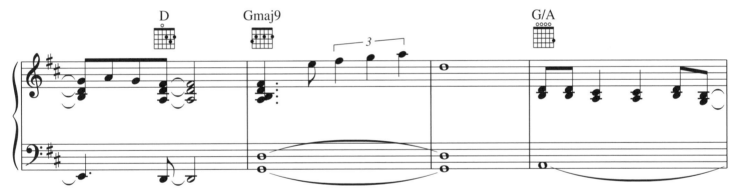

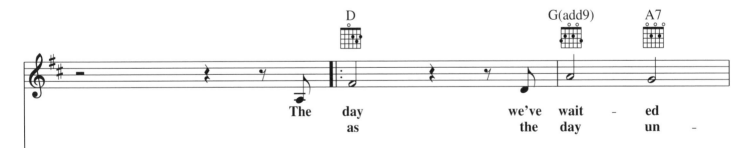

The day we've wait - ed
as the day un -

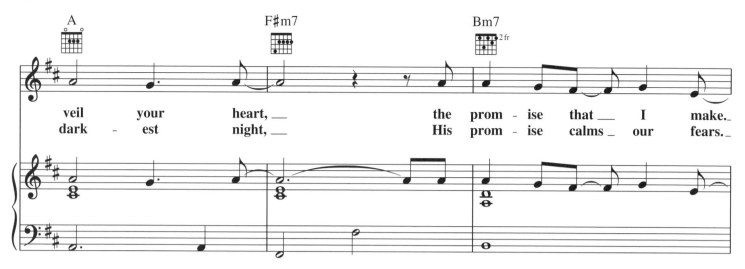

veil   your   heart, ___   the prom - ise that ___ I   make. __
dark - est   night, ___   His prom - ise calms __ our   fears. __

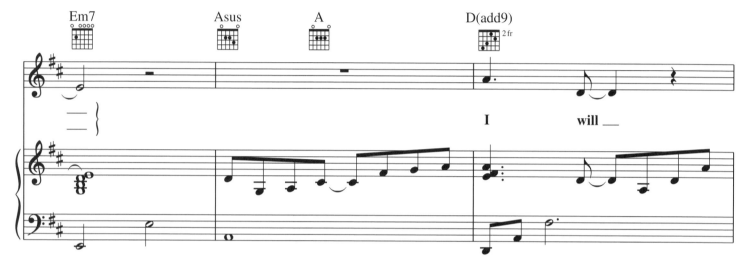

I   will ___

have   you __   and   I   will __   hold _____ you   un -

til _____ the   end _____ of ___ time.

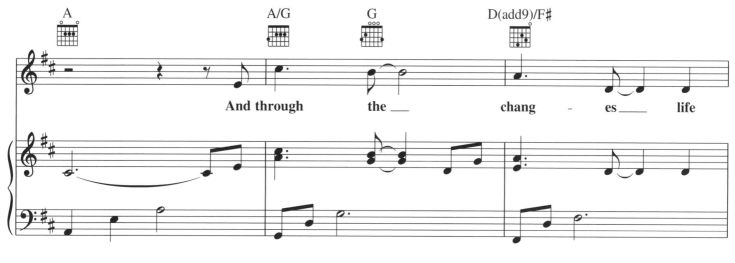

And through the ___ chang - es ___ life

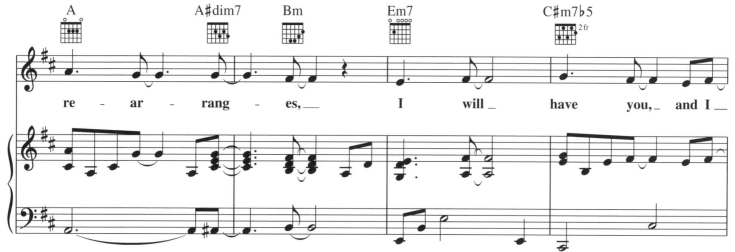

re - ar - rang - es, ___ I will ___ have you, ___ and I ___

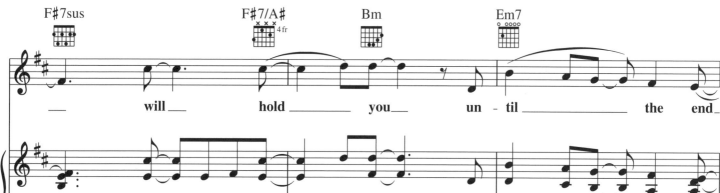

___ will ___ hold ___ you ___ un - til ___ the end ___

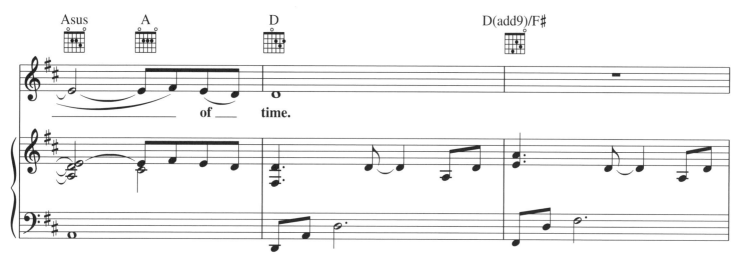

___ of ___ time.

un - til _____ the end _____

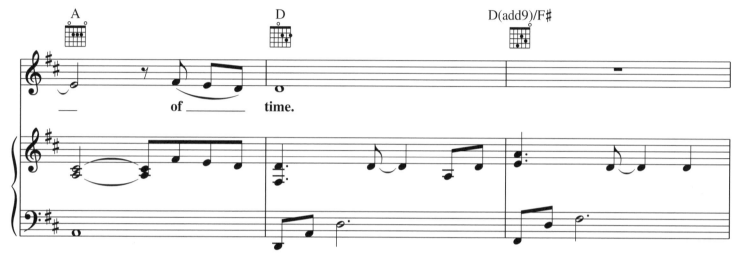

of _____ time.

HAL•LEONARD WEDDING ESSENTIALS

INCLUDES REFERENCE CD

The Wedding Essentials series is a great resource for wedding musicians, featuring beautiful arrangements for a variety of instruments. Each book includes a reference CD to help couples choose the perfect songs for their wedding ceremony or reception.

Christian Wedding Favorites

Answered Prayer • God Causes All Things to Grow • God Knew That I Needed You • Household of Faith • I Will Be Here • If You Could See What I See • Love Will Be Our Home • Seekers of Your Heart • This Day • 'Til the End of Time.
00311941 P/V/G $16.99

Contemporary Wedding Ballads

Beautiful in My Eyes • Bless the Broken Road • Endless Love • (Everything I Do) I Do It for You • From This Moment On • Have I Told You Lately • Here and Now • Love of a Lifetime • More Than Words • When You Say You Love Me.
00311942 P/V/G $16.99

Love Songs for Weddings

Grow Old with Me • Here, There and Everywhere • If • Longer • Part of My Heart • Valentine • We've Only Just Begun • The Wedding Song • You and I • You Raise Me Up.
00311943 Piano Solo $16.99

Service Music for Weddings

Processionals, Recessionals, Lighting of the Unity Candle
Allegro maestoso • Amazing Grace • Ave Maria • Canon in D • Jesu, Joy of Man's Desiring • Jupiter (Chorale Theme) • O Perfect Love • Ode to Joy • Rondeau • Trumpet Voluntary.
00311944 Piano Solo $14.99

Wedding Guitar Solos

All I Ask of You • Gabriel's Oboe • Grow Old with Me • Hallelujah • Here, There and Everywhere • More Than Words • Sunrise, Sunset • Wedding Song (There Is Love) • When I Fall in Love • You Raise Me Up.
00701335 Guitar Solo $16.99

Wedding Vocal Solos

Grow Old with Me • I Swear • In My Life • Longer • The Promise (I'll Never Say Goodbye) • Someone Like You • Sunrise, Sunset • Till There Was You • Time After Time • We've Only Just Begun.
00311945 High Voice $16.99
00311946 Low Voice $16.99

Worship for Weddings

Be Unto Your Name • Broken and Beautiful • Center • He Is Here • Here and Now • Holy Ground • How Beautiful • Listen to Our Hearts • Today (As for Me and My House).
00311949 P/V/G $16.99